<u>Dedication</u>

This one's for all my root veg.

Wherever on Earth you reside.

Thakek loop

i had no body
but techno in my ear
motorbike a'ride me.

some cigs
             feeling queer.

i rode into mountains.
and there I felt free.
i had or needed nothing
a moment just for me.

"If you're going to try go all the way.
Otherwise don't even start"

Charles Bukowski

Quack

I came up on a duck today.
it rivaled me some tun.

Splat at me
it shook and spray
        unbridled me
              an' some.

Man #366

Sat down in a chair
not even your own
leg swollen bandaged
no place to call home.

Bus honks besides ya
there's little to wait
when waiting moves sideways
to nothing that's great.

Rest eyes asleep man
tucked up sat there
hope you're at peace now
no thoughts to despair.

Sleep tight little man
for now you can dream
of a time things were different
of a time things would gleam.

Thakek loop

i had no body
but techno in my ear
motorbike a'ride me.

some cigs
          feeling queer.

i rode into mountains.
and there I felt free.
i had or needed nothing
a moment just for me.

Andy Pandy pudding in eye

8th in line
can't commit no crime
Will someone. Somewhere

Listen
       this time.

With trafficked girls
sure 'over' age
a smudge an' push

             our accolade.

Please hail all thoughts
before the crown
for they're not yours
             so settle down.

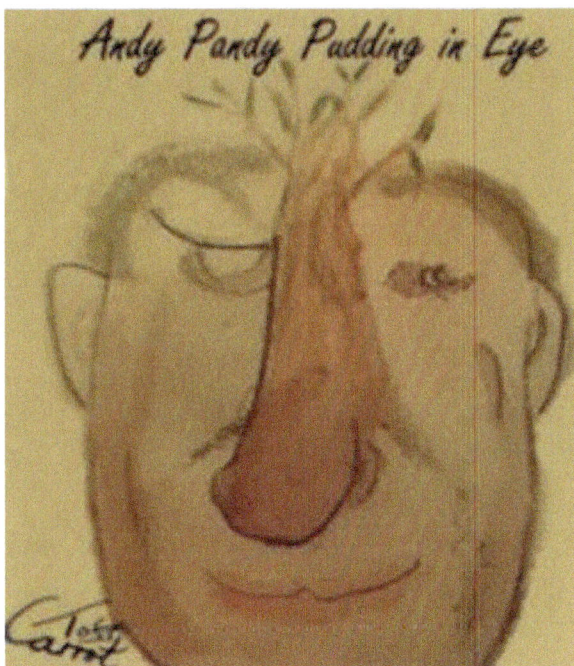

Andy Pandy Pudding in Eye

From Pope to nun

she belongs to the catholic church
            hollowed in his name
                    will to be done.

As though will was

                        not

for everyone.

K-hore

Honk nostril
up now
         to my vein
Ketamine
is just pure pain.

Minds talk
around me
         souls rejoice
incontinence
it just destroys.

A.

35. Kid 17.
She's almost that age where things could have been
Why'd Dad die?
                        at night you still scream.

Then mum followed too. And now brother's unseen.
He passed the exams, but police try to glean
6 thousand to enter.
                        this country's obscene.

Try to survive.
Just waiting on wait.
Let down by partners.
                        recovery quake.

Yet your heart thaws on forwards.
Perhaps it's a must.
Faith on in strangers, a fate you can trust.
Why don't you hate the ephemeral dust?
When I'm glugging beers. A freedom unjust.

I'd help if I could. I'm not sure that I can.
When I'm a drop in a river
When I'm just a grain of sand.

Beggin' Tom'

So look at me with face of doubt.
Yet souk from me; 1 pound to clout.

One thousand days I slept beneath.
those Swedish trees. Now Laos conplete.
No embassy. I would not score.

Yet hostel bathroom. Face deplore.
I did not mean to bump to you
though I enjoyed.
How your face grew.
For it was red.
And not through heat.
Perhaps because those lies you pleat.

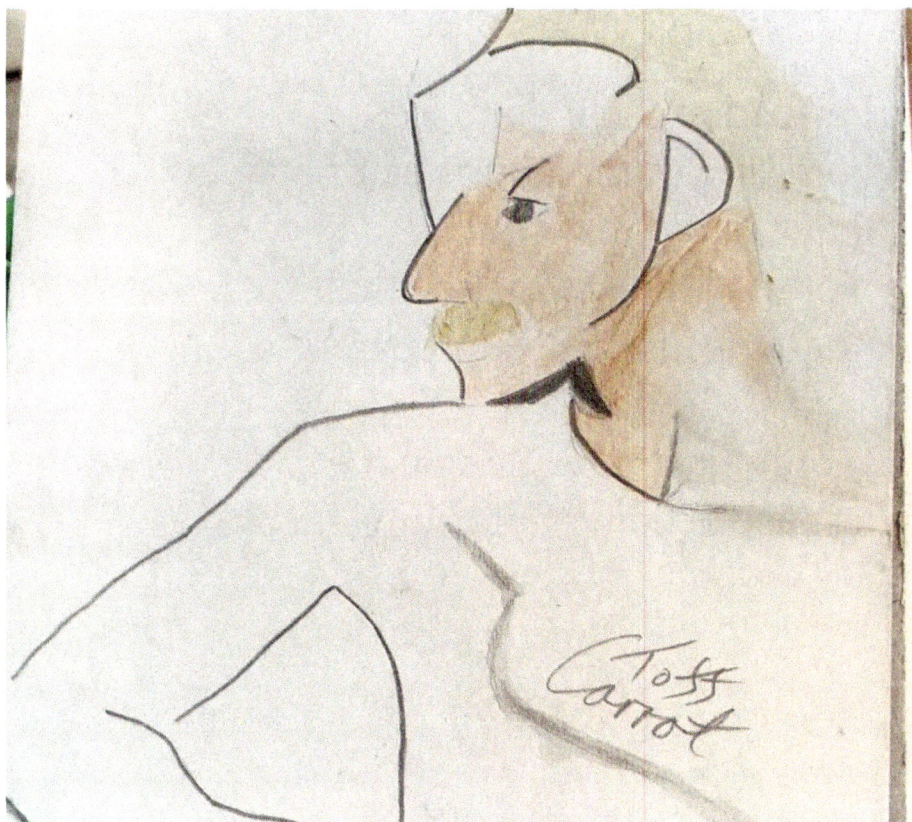

A stained tablecloth

The knife was set off cue
she say.

Perfection there done in.
Perhaps your madness can't convey
that beauty lies within.
Not with nails or perfect hair
nor table setting we prepare.

It only lied between you me
a space needing deformity.

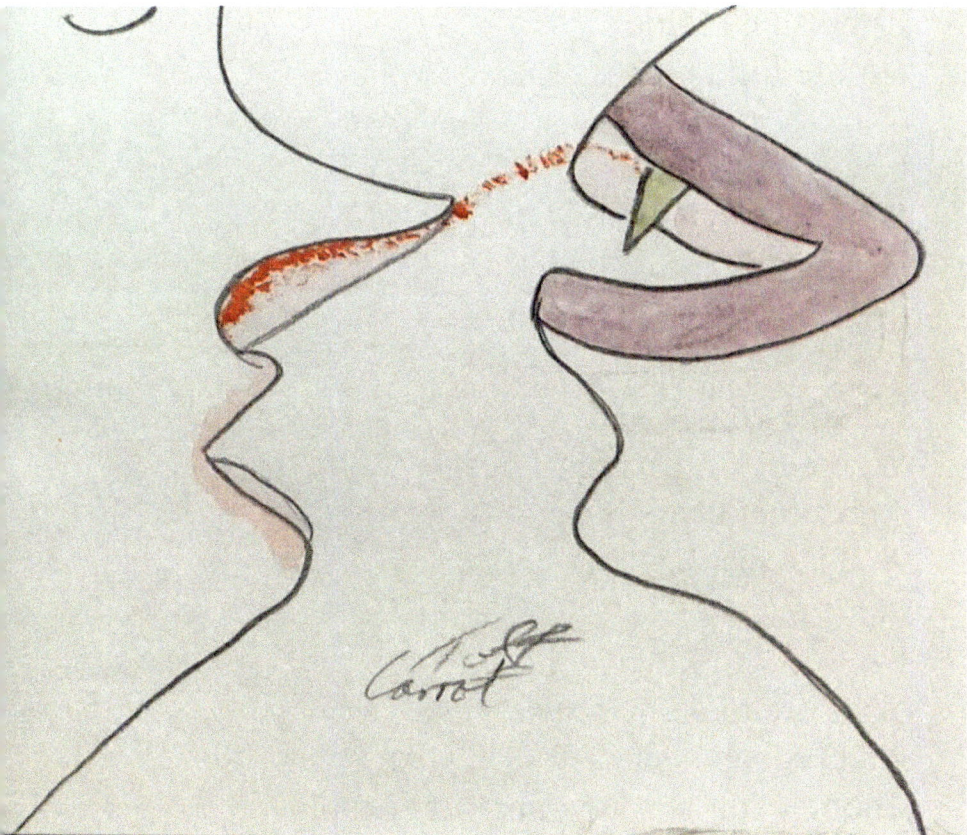

Carrot

Sticks and stones

There you are
just a flea
an' sum fur
Rubbish n rubble
No life for a purr.

I'm sorry lil kitten
Didn' ask to be born
Hiding under that box
From a world full of scorn.

I'd take you away
Where the traffic don't beep
And street vendors pet
And I'd just feed you treats.

I'm sorry lil kitten
Your life looks so cruel
And probably short
Though you're too young for school.

Sorry lil kitten
Didn' do those things
And thinking you now
will do nothing to bring.

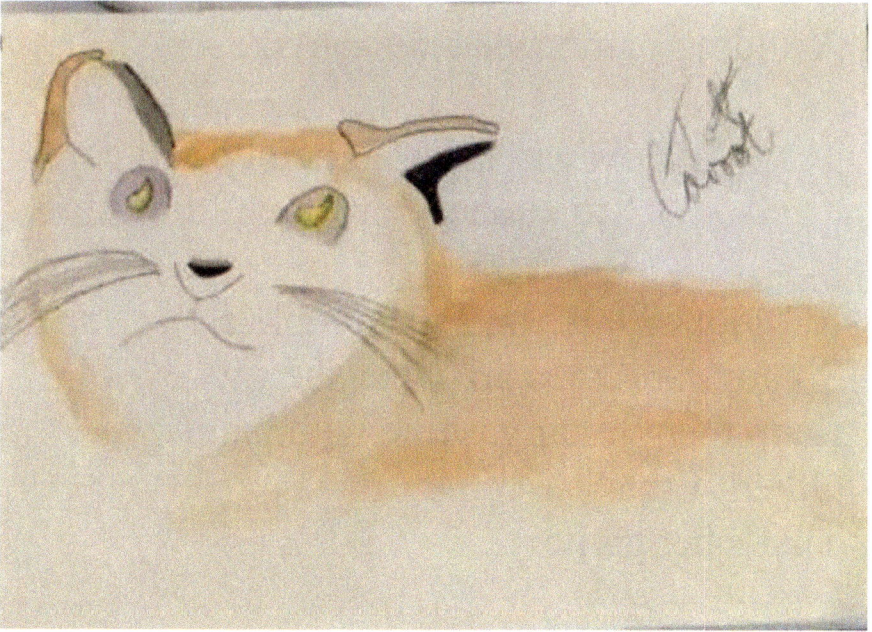

Olga

Came from Russia endowned with frown.
Her lover lost; heart upside down
Begin to move.
But not to chase
Avoiding pain's what she partakes.

How can I run? When I don't care?
I'll open bar for child welfare.

But money talks and souls replete
So boys and men are what she eats.
Keep them hungry, some with pain.
Others Yaba.
That's her game.

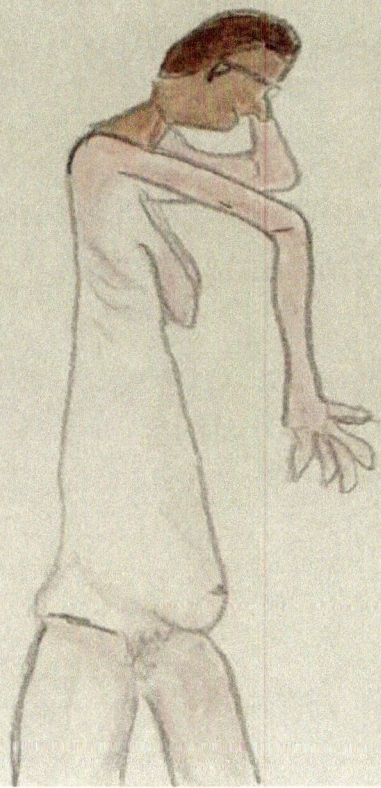

Reflections from a noise I heard in a bush

A duck quacked at me today
it made me jump through skin.
Hidden in a bush it lay
                          awaiting rival kin.

The children laughed at me and say
you're not a man; nufin.

Perhaps a scare crow's frightened way
is how i shall fit in.

Peter Pan Syndrome

Run to an island far away
from hooks and demoned
       responsibilitay.

Age is just a number
conceived to trap.
Lost boys on an island
don't need no map.
shaggin', sniffin'
after Gloryed Days.

If only you knew it's called a
          Holiday.

Bus lady

She looked at me.
As rivers fold.
from mountain
to a bed.

I looked away
deservingly.
in shadow's light
instead.

My little Vase

Cracked down one side
where the Flowers grew.
Held self together
without need for glue.

My little vase
holding nothing now.
No stagnant water
or remnants of though.

Fill up my vase
a drink does the job.
Cigarettes plenty
some drugs, be a slob.

No little vase
there's simply no choice.
Must sit there empty
till a sun you'll rejoice.

Someone I'll never marry

Came from France, Tonight by self.
Met me with a smile and that couple helped.
'Take one look how she looks at ye'
'You're in there mate give her one from me'

She came back. Seclusion we sought.
But a drunken Brit weren't what she bought.

A kiss denied.
An empty bed.
It's 3am.
With vomit ahead.

EO

Loved quite short
forgotten quite long.
a memory haunts
Till you belong.

Run,
  run,
    run
now
    can't forget.

Sobreity's sanctuary's
your regret.

Untitled.

"You failed selecting pronouns Dr Bones."

Was't it ill or fur?

If choice for him,
or his or her

A
  M
    I
      am.

It will do Sir?
             Or mrs…? Miss?
                         Peculiar….?

So nouns are names.
             Identity.

       And without pro I shall be free.

Mouth open knees bent

I pledge allegiance to my King
for God above Cast down his ring.
I take my knee before his Crown
twas not his fault, it wast hand down.

Britain's Great, so it can't change;
These are the rules, don't rearrange.
We're not born equal, some should rule
our politicians, different schools.
I know my place,
as so should thee
I heard that's called democracy.

Check in
       Call in
              Out my name.

Scratch that itch
           don't mind the blame.

It's all happened
          so ignore.

Avoidant
       leanings
            where you're drawn.

untitled

for the many
For the few.
The much and such have nuff to do.

Wealth will trickle
       it will fall
       or set like treacle
              above us all.

**My skin is a story,
its cracks filled with gold.**

Sliced my skin
twas all the same
sowed back
           together
                undone.

A scar's wrought fracture
memories blame
in-perfections strengthen some.

I came
        I saw
                I plundered.

Not if
      but
            thought for self.

For if
      on earth
                I wandered.

That
      sanctuary
             might help.

running late. important date

Tik
    Tok

            Attention
                         Drop.

Can not focus
        can not stop.

The world surround was filled with greed

        for dopamine addiction sprees.

high. No

flies   one

Noise   there to see it.

Choice   will free it.

ran   dance

dry.   Only

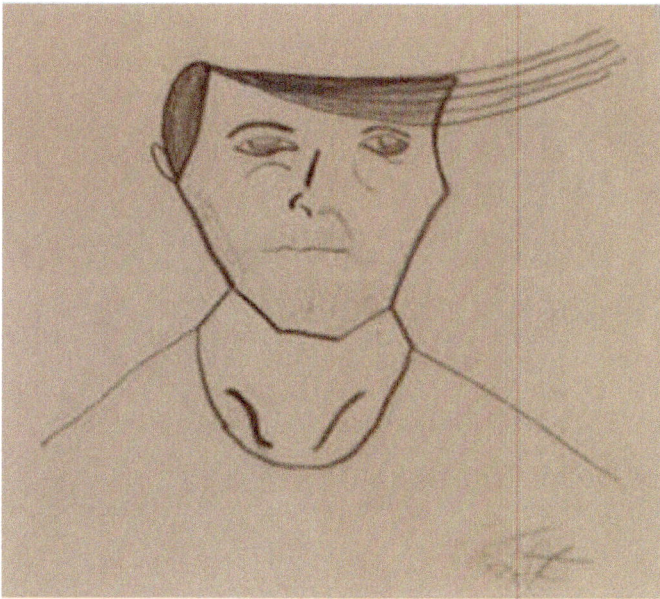

A Garden of Judas

When farmer said...
                        'ere parsnips lay'

I shed a tear within'

for Carrots are what I display   One
hangs above my chin.

our closest friends can still betray
An' turn their backs wit' grin
for farmer did this just for pay.
I can't forgiven him.

8TH

To fold a fitted sheet?

I made my bed today
to stop me going in
It wasn't much
I have to say
but hard when feelin' grim

I ran outside today
though after ten I stopped
I didn't stretch
was quite foul fetched
and went home with a hop.

I didn't try today
there was such little point
with curtains shut
sat on my but
I asked myself well what?

You smiled at me today
it bounced right off my shin
just go fuck off
my disdain scoffed
I've made the bed i'm in.

Today my bed's a mess
and though I didn' stretch
my focus lay
not on my way
for that I'm feeling blessed.

Yin and Yang

Parsnips' leave a sour taste
and stomach feelin' grim.

They stink an' rot
our children's brains
and end all life within.

Carrot taste is sweet and luff
digestive aid it be.

It help the mind
an' eyes as well
so reality
you'll see.

FACE THE FACTS

IF YOU DESIRE A **PARSNIP**

FOR YOUR NEIGHBOUR

VOTE LABOUR

IF YOU ARE ALREADY BURDONED
WITH ONE

VOTE **TORY**

The Conservatives once in Office, will bring
up to date the **Ministry of Repatriation**, to
Speed up the return of home-going and
expelled immigrants.

Bisto

Freedom.
It came to me
I moved through life
like fresh gravy.

Not with thickness
nor with thin.

For I moved softly.
Took it in.

I had no wants
nor desires
Sat patiently.
no need Acquire.

A Destination

At night it's dark an' then it rains
don' like these wood's. They feel quite
strange.

                                        Meet old man.
                                  shelter in home.

he live in cave,
 it all he own.
                  Tell my story,
parsnip defeat
            how drawin' keep my soul replete.

He tell me of a place call' Tate
where art displays of those who great.

I ask him where now does it lay?
In LunDan, Town; quite far away.

So now I march with one sole track
Display my work.
                          Get farmer back!

Untitled

Don't look for way out
                don't look for discretion.

For if there is doubt
                there's always a lesson.

a Carrot never Forgets

As a boy I had to learn
Scare them crows
Me gotta earn.

Stood through dreary
shallow nights.
Awaitin' spring and carrots' might.

Saw them sprout. But it weren't true.
A field of parsnips! Gimmie the blues.
Farmer 'tray me. Pack my bags.
What else to do when feel so sad?

Now wanderin is where I lay
No where home, no bed or hay.

So tell these stories, this I must
for outside art keep heart from rust.

About the author

Carrot Toff spent his formative years raising and tending his rural patch. Loyal to his crop he found himself at ease with the simple life of a veg grower, finding himself more attuned to the seasons than the day-to-day troubles which beset those elsewhere.

Alas his commitment to the yield was soon betrayed. Inspecting the shoots in Spring something appeared awry. With the cost of living crisis in full fury Farmer had decided to plant parsnips instead. A biennial plant, sure to appease the farm's purse strings. Aghast, Carrot Toff abandoned his patch and began to wander. He now finds himself wedded to the road, his time spent documenting tales, both past and present.

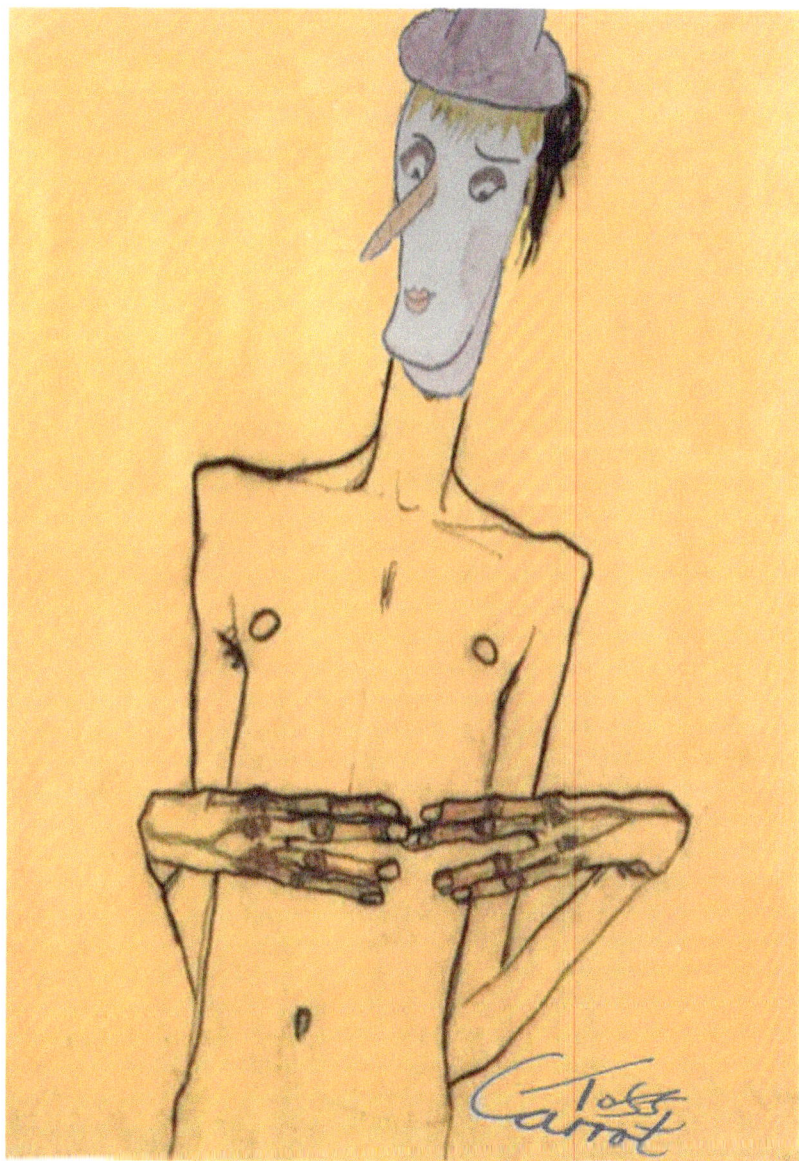

Printed in Great Britain
by Amazon